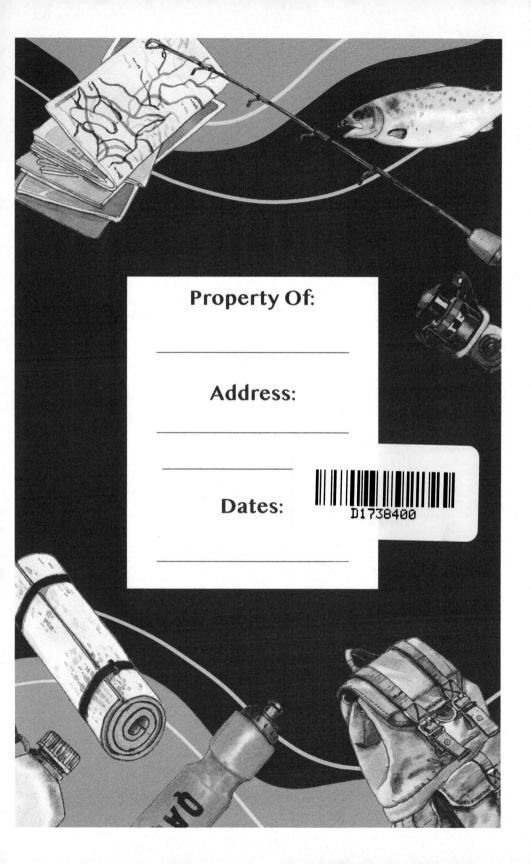

Property Of:

_____

Address:

_____

_____

Dates:

_____

D1738400

How to Use This Logbook

Each campground has a Trip # in the top right corner of the first page of that campground's section. Note the Trip # and come back to the Campground Index and fill in the Campground/Location, Date and your Overall Rating.

There are four pages for each campground so you can note the details for each place, along with special memories, friends, and other important details.

In the back of the book, there are two checklists to help you with your tent camping packing and RV prep. There is space on each checklist for you to write important items to you that aren't listed.

When complete, this log book will be a fantastic reference for you to choose which campsites to revisit and will be a keepsake full of memories that you will treasure forever.

Enjoy every second of your camping adventures! Maybe I'll see you somewhere on your journeys.

Campground Index

Trip #	Campground/Location	Date	Overall Rating
1			☆☆☆☆☆
2			☆☆☆☆☆
3			☆☆☆☆☆
4			☆☆☆☆☆
5			☆☆☆☆☆
6			☆☆☆☆☆
7			☆☆☆☆☆
8			☆☆☆☆☆
9			☆☆☆☆☆
10			☆☆☆☆☆
11			☆☆☆☆☆
12			☆☆☆☆☆
13			☆☆☆☆☆
14			☆☆☆☆☆
15			☆☆☆☆☆
16			☆☆☆☆☆
17			☆☆☆☆☆
18			☆☆☆☆☆
19			☆☆☆☆☆
20			☆☆☆☆☆
21			☆☆☆☆☆
22			☆☆☆☆☆
23			☆☆☆☆☆
24			☆☆☆☆☆
25			☆☆☆☆☆
26			☆☆☆☆☆
27			☆☆☆☆☆
28			☆☆☆☆☆
29			☆☆☆☆☆
30			☆☆☆☆☆

Notes, Lists, Drawings, Photos

Dates: _____ **to** _____
Campground: _____
Traveled From: _____ **Miles:** _____ **Time:** _____
Fees: _____ **Pull-Through** ☐ **Back-In** ☐

Hookups:

FHU	☐	W/E Only	☐
50 & 30 Amp	☐	30 Amp Only	☐
Dry Camp	☐	Dumping	☐
Notes:			

Restrooms/Showers:

Flush Toilets Yes ☐ No ☐	
Showers Yes ☐ No ☐ Free ☐ Paid ☐	
Enough Hot Water Yes ☐ No ☐	
Cleanliness:	

Amenities:

Pool	☐	Hot Tub	☐	Game Room	☐	Laundry	☐
Restaurant	☐	Pet-Friendly	☐	Dog Park	☐	Playground	☐
Shuffleboard	☐	Hiking	☐	Boating	☐	Fishing	☐
Horses	☐	Fitness Room	☐	Store	☐	Ice	☐
Firewood	☐		☐		☐		☐
Notes:							

Site Details for Site # ____:

RV Pad		Size/Access		Shade/Noise		Picnic Area	
Level	☐	Small	☐	No Shade	☐	Fire Ring	☐
Not Level	☐	Medium	☐	Partial Shade	☐	Fires Allowed	☐
Paved	☐	Large	☐	Full Shade	☐	Picnic Table	☐
Grass	☐	Tight Turns	☐	Quiet	☐	Good View	☐
Dirt	☐	Low Trees	☐	Light Noise	☐	Private	☐
Other	☐	Poor Roads	☐	Very Noisy	☐	No Privacy	☐

Safety:

Felt Very Safe ☐   Moderately Safe ☐   Felt Unsafe ☐

Wi-Fi:

Wi-Fi Available	☐
Poor Signal	☐
Good Signal	☐
Excellent Signal	☐
Notes:	

Notes:

_____
_____
_____
_____
_____
_____
_____

Who Was With Us? _____

_____

_____

People We Met: _____

_____

_____

Fun Things We Did: _____

_____

_____

Things to Remember For Next Time: _____

_____

_____

_____

_____

Favorite Memories: _____

_____

_____

_____

_____

_____

_____

All About The Scenery: _____

_____

_____

_____

_____

_____

Area Around The Campground:

What Was the Weather Like? _____
_____
_____

Sightseeing/Activities:	Distance:	Fees/Contact Info:
_____	_____	_____
_____	_____	_____
_____	_____	_____
_____	_____	_____
_____	_____	_____

Nearby Restaurants: _____
_____
_____

Nearby Groceries: _____
_____
_____

Overall Thoughts About This Campground (Do you want
to revisit? Site # You Want to Reserve? Important Things
To Remember, etc.)

_____
_____
_____
_____
_____
_____
_____

Notes, Lists, Drawings, Photos

Dates: _____ **to** _____

Campground: _____

Traveled From: _____ **Miles:** _____ **Time:** _____

Fees: _____ **Pull-Through** ☐ **Back-In** ☐

Hookups:

FHU	☐	W/E Only	☐
50 & 30 Amp	☐	30 Amp Only	☐
Dry Camp	☐	Dumping	☐
Notes:			

Restrooms/Showers:

Flush Toilets Yes ☐ No ☐	
Showers Yes ☐ No ☐ Free ☐ Paid ☐	
Enough Hot Water Yes ☐ No ☐	
Cleanliness:	

Amenities:

Pool	☐	Hot Tub	☐	Game Room	☐	Laundry	☐
Restaurant	☐	Pet-Friendly	☐	Dog Park	☐	Playground	☐
Shuffleboard	☐	Hiking	☐	Boating	☐	Fishing	☐
Horses	☐	Fitness Room	☐	Store	☐	Ice	☐
Firewood	☐		☐		☐		☐
Notes:							

Site Details for Site # ____:

RV Pad		Size/Access		Shade/Noise		Picnic Area	
Level	☐	Small	☐	No Shade	☐	Fire Ring	☐
Not Level	☐	Medium	☐	Partial Shade	☐	Fires Allowed	☐
Paved	☐	Large	☐	Full Shade	☐	Picnic Table	☐
Grass	☐	Tight Turns	☐	Quiet	☐	Good View	☐
Dirt	☐	Low Trees	☐	Light Noise	☐	Private	☐
Other	☐	Poor Roads	☐	Very Noisy	☐	No Privacy	☐

Safety:

Felt Very Safe ☐   Moderately Safe ☐   Felt Unsafe ☐

Wi-Fi:

Wi-Fi Available	☐
Poor Signal	☐
Good Signal	☐
Excellent Signal	☐
Notes:	

Notes:

_____
_____
_____
_____
_____
_____
_____

Who Was With Us? _____
_____
_____

People We Met: _____
_____
_____

Fun Things We Did: _____
_____
_____

Things to Remember For Next Time: _____
_____
_____
_____
_____

Favorite Memories: _____
_____
_____
_____
_____
_____
_____
_____

All About The Scenery: _____
_____
_____
_____
_____
_____

Area Around The Campground:

What Was the Weather Like? _____
_____
_____

Sightseeing/Activities:	Distance:	Fees/Contact Info:
_____	_____	_____
_____	_____	_____
_____	_____	_____
_____	_____	_____
_____	_____	_____

Nearby Restaurants: _____
_____
_____

Nearby Groceries: _____
_____
_____

Overall Thoughts About This Campground (Do you want
to revisit? Site # You Want to Reserve? Important Things
To Remember, etc.)

_____
_____
_____
_____
_____
_____
_____
_____

Notes, Lists, Drawings, Photos

Dates: _____ **to** _____

Campground: _____

Traveled From: _____ **Miles:** _____ **Time:** _____

Fees: _____ **Pull-Through** ☐ **Back-In** ☐

Hookups:

FHU	☐	W/E Only	☐
50 & 30 Amp	☐	30 Amp Only	☐
Dry Camp	☐	Dumping	☐
Notes:			

Restrooms/Showers:

Flush Toilets	Yes ☐	No ☐
Showers Yes ☐	No ☐ Free ☐	Paid ☐
Enough Hot Water	Yes ☐	No ☐
Cleanliness:		

Amenities:

Pool	☐	Hot Tub	☐	Game Room	☐	Laundry	☐
Restaurant	☐	Pet-Friendly	☐	Dog Park	☐	Playground	☐
Shuffleboard	☐	Hiking	☐	Boating	☐	Fishing	☐
Horses	☐	Fitness Room	☐	Store	☐	Ice	☐
Firewood	☐		☐		☐		☐
Notes:							

Site Details for Site # _____:

RV Pad		Size/Access		Shade/Noise		Picnic Area	
Level	☐	Small	☐	No Shade	☐	Fire Ring	☐
Not Level	☐	Medium	☐	Partial Shade	☐	Fires Allowed	☐
Paved	☐	Large	☐	Full Shade	☐	Picnic Table	☐
Grass	☐	Tight Turns	☐	Quiet	☐	Good View	☐
Dirt	☐	Low Trees	☐	Light Noise	☐	Private	☐
Other	☐	Poor Roads	☐	Very Noisy	☐	No Privacy	☐

Safety:

Felt Very Safe ☐   Moderately Safe ☐   Felt Unsafe ☐

Wi-Fi:

Wi-Fi Available	☐
Poor Signal	☐
Good Signal	☐
Excellent Signal	☐
Notes:	

Notes:

_____
_____
_____
_____
_____
_____
_____

Who Was With Us? _____

_____

_____

People We Met: _____

_____

_____

Fun Things We Did: _____

_____

_____

Things to Remember For Next Time: _____

_____

_____

_____

_____

Favorite Memories: _____

_____

_____

_____

_____

_____

_____

_____

All About The Scenery: _____

_____

_____

_____

_____

_____

Area Around The Campground:

What Was the Weather Like? _____
_____
_____

Sightseeing/Activities:	Distance:	Fees/Contact Info:
_____	_____	_____
_____	_____	_____
_____	_____	_____
_____	_____	_____
_____	_____	_____

Nearby Restaurants: _____
_____
_____

Nearby Groceries: _____
_____
_____

Overall Thoughts About This Campground (Do you want
to revisit? Site # You Want to Reserve? Important Things
To Remember, etc.)

_____
_____
_____
_____
_____
_____
_____

Notes, Lists, Drawings, Photos

Dates: _____ **to** _____

Campground: _____

Traveled From: _____ **Miles:** _____ **Time:** _____

Fees: _____ **Pull-Through** ☐ **Back-In** ☐

Hookups:

FHU	☐	W/E Only	☐
50 & 30 Amp	☐	30 Amp Only	☐
Dry Camp	☐	Dumping	☐
Notes:			

Restrooms/Showers:

Flush Toilets	Yes ☐ No ☐
Showers Yes ☐ No ☐ Free ☐ Paid ☐	
Enough Hot Water	Yes ☐ No ☐
Cleanliness:	

Amenities:

Pool	☐	Hot Tub	☐	Game Room	☐	Laundry	☐
Restaurant	☐	Pet-Friendly	☐	Dog Park	☐	Playground	☐
Shuffleboard	☐	Hiking	☐	Boating	☐	Fishing	☐
Horses	☐	Fitness Room	☐	Store	☐	Ice	☐
Firewood	☐		☐		☐		☐
Notes:							

Site Details for Site # _____:

RV Pad		Size/Access		Shade/Noise		Picnic Area	
Level	☐	Small	☐	No Shade	☐	Fire Ring	☐
Not Level	☐	Medium	☐	Partial Shade	☐	Fires Allowed	☐
Paved	☐	Large	☐	Full Shade	☐	Picnic Table	☐
Grass	☐	Tight Turns	☐	Quiet	☐	Good View	☐
Dirt	☐	Low Trees	☐	Light Noise	☐	Private	☐
Other	☐	Poor Roads	☐	Very Noisy	☐	No Privacy	☐

Safety:

Felt Very Safe ☐   Moderately Safe ☐   Felt Unsafe ☐

Wi-Fi:

Wi-Fi Available	☐
Poor Signal	☐
Good Signal	☐
Excellent Signal	☐
Notes:	

Notes:

_____
_____
_____
_____
_____
_____
_____

Who Was With Us? _____
_____
_____

People We Met: _____
_____
_____

Fun Things We Did: _____
_____
_____

Things to Remember For Next Time: _____
_____
_____
_____
_____

Favorite Memories: _____
_____
_____
_____
_____
_____
_____
_____

All About The Scenery: _____
_____
_____
_____
_____
_____

Area Around The Campground:

What Was the Weather Like? _____
_____
_____

Sightseeing/Activities:	Distance:	Fees/Contact Info:
_____	_____	_____
_____	_____	_____
_____	_____	_____
_____	_____	_____
_____	_____	_____

Nearby Restaurants: _____
_____
_____

Nearby Groceries: _____
_____
_____

Overall Thoughts About This Campground (Do you want
to revisit? Site # You Want to Reserve? Important Things
To Remember, etc.)

_____
_____
_____
_____
_____
_____
_____

Notes, Lists, Drawings, Photos

Trip #5

Dates: _____ **to** _____

Campground: _____

Traveled From: _____ **Miles:** _____ **Time:** _____

Fees: _____ **Pull-Through** ☐ **Back-In** ☐

Hookups:

FHU	☐	W/E Only	☐
50 & 30 Amp	☐	30 Amp Only	☐
Dry Camp	☐	Dumping	☐
Notes:			

Restrooms/Showers:

Flush Toilets Yes ☐ No ☐	
Showers Yes ☐ No ☐ Free ☐ Paid ☐	
Enough Hot Water Yes ☐ No ☐	
Cleanliness:	

Amenities:

Pool	☐	Hot Tub	☐	Game Room	☐	Laundry	☐
Restaurant	☐	Pet-Friendly	☐	Dog Park	☐	Playground	☐
Shuffleboard	☐	Hiking	☐	Boating	☐	Fishing	☐
Horses	☐	Fitness Room	☐	Store	☐	Ice	☐
Firewood	☐		☐		☐		☐
Notes:							

Site Details for Site # _____:

RV Pad		Size/Access		Shade/Noise		Picnic Area	
Level	☐	Small	☐	No Shade	☐	Fire Ring	☐
Not Level	☐	Medium	☐	Partial Shade	☐	Fires Allowed	☐
Paved	☐	Large	☐	Full Shade	☐	Picnic Table	☐
Grass	☐	Tight Turns	☐	Quiet	☐	Good View	☐
Dirt	☐	Low Trees	☐	Light Noise	☐	Private	☐
Other	☐	Poor Roads	☐	Very Noisy	☐	No Privacy	☐

Safety:

Felt Very Safe ☐   Moderately Safe ☐   Felt Unsafe ☐

Wi-Fi:

Wi-Fi Available	☐
Poor Signal	☐
Good Signal	☐
Excellent Signal	☐
Notes:	

Notes:

_____
_____
_____
_____
_____
_____
_____
_____

Who Was With Us?_____

_____

_____

People We Met: _____

_____

_____

Fun Things We Did: _____

_____

_____

Things to Remember For Next Time: _____

_____

_____

_____

Favorite Memories: _____

_____

_____

_____

_____

_____

_____

All About The Scenery: _____

_____

_____

_____

_____

_____

Area Around The Campground:

What Was the Weather Like? _____
_____
_____

Sightseeing/Activities:	Distance:	Fees/Contact Info:
_____	_____	_____
_____	_____	_____
_____	_____	_____
_____	_____	_____
_____	_____	_____

Nearby Restaurants: _____
_____
_____

Nearby Groceries: _____
_____
_____

Overall Thoughts About This Campground (Do you want
to revisit? Site # You Want to Reserve? Important Things
To Remember, etc.)

_____
_____
_____
_____
_____
_____
_____

Notes, Lists, Drawings, Photos

Dates: _____ **to** _____

Campground: _____

Traveled From: _____ **Miles:** _____ **Time:** _____

Fees: _____ **Pull-Through** ☐ **Back-In** ☐

Hookups:

FHU	☐	W/E Only	☐
50 & 30 Amp	☐	30 Amp Only	☐
Dry Camp	☐	Dumping	☐
Notes:			

Restrooms/Showers:

Flush Toilets	Yes ☐	No ☐
Showers Yes ☐ No ☐	Free ☐	Paid ☐
Enough Hot Water Yes ☐	No ☐	
Cleanliness:		

Amenities:

Pool	☐	Hot Tub	☐	Game Room	☐	Laundry	☐
Restaurant	☐	Pet-Friendly	☐	Dog Park	☐	Playground	☐
Shuffleboard	☐	Hiking	☐	Boating	☐	Fishing	☐
Horses	☐	Fitness Room	☐	Store	☐	Ice	☐
Firewood	☐		☐		☐		☐
Notes:							

Site Details for Site # _____:

RV Pad		Size/Access		Shade/Noise		Picnic Area	
Level	☐	Small	☐	No Shade	☐	Fire Ring	☐
Not Level	☐	Medium	☐	Partial Shade	☐	Fires Allowed	☐
Paved	☐	Large	☐	Full Shade	☐	Picnic Table	☐
Grass	☐	Tight Turns	☐	Quiet	☐	Good View	☐
Dirt	☐	Low Trees	☐	Light Noise	☐	Private	☐
Other	☐	Poor Roads	☐	Very Noisy	☐	No Privacy	☐

Safety:

Felt Very Safe ☐   Moderately Safe ☐   Felt Unsafe ☐

Wi-Fi:

Wi-Fi Available	☐
Poor Signal	☐
Good Signal	☐
Excellent Signal	☐
Notes:	

Notes:

_____
_____
_____
_____
_____
_____
_____

Who Was With Us? _____
_____
_____

People We Met: _____
_____
_____

Fun Things We Did: _____
_____
_____

Things to Remember For Next Time: _____
_____
_____
_____
_____

Favorite Memories: _____
_____
_____
_____
_____
_____
_____
_____

All About The Scenery: _____
_____
_____
_____
_____
_____

Area Around The Campground:

What Was the Weather Like? _____

_____

_____

Sightseeing/Activities:	Distance:	Fees/Contact Info:
_____	_____	_____
_____	_____	_____
_____	_____	_____
_____	_____	_____
_____	_____	_____

Nearby Restaurants: _____

_____

_____

Nearby Groceries: _____

_____

_____

Overall Thoughts About This Campground (Do you want to revisit? Site # You Want to Reserve? Important Things To Remember, etc.)

_____

_____

_____

_____

_____

_____

_____

Notes, Lists, Drawings, Photos

Dates: _____ to _____

Campground: _____

Traveled From: _____ Miles: _____ Time: _____

Fees: _____ Pull-Through ☐ Back-In ☐

Hookups:

FHU	☐	W/E Only	☐
50 & 30 Amp	☐	30 Amp Only	☐
Dry Camp	☐	Dumping	☐
Notes:			

Restrooms/Showers:

Flush Toilets	Yes ☐	No ☐
Showers Yes ☐ No ☐	Free ☐	Paid ☐
Enough Hot Water	Yes ☐	No ☐
Cleanliness:		

Amenities:

Pool	☐	Hot Tub	☐	Game Room	☐	Laundry	☐
Restaurant	☐	Pet-Friendly	☐	Dog Park	☐	Playground	☐
Shuffleboard	☐	Hiking	☐	Boating	☐	Fishing	☐
Horses	☐	Fitness Room	☐	Store	☐	Ice	☐
Firewood	☐		☐		☐		☐
Notes:							

Site Details for Site # ____:

RV Pad		Size/Access		Shade/Noise		Picnic Area	
Level	☐	Small	☐	No Shade	☐	Fire Ring	☐
Not Level	☐	Medium	☐	Partial Shade	☐	Fires Allowed	☐
Paved	☐	Large	☐	Full Shade	☐	Picnic Table	☐
Grass	☐	Tight Turns	☐	Quiet	☐	Good View	☐
Dirt	☐	Low Trees	☐	Light Noise	☐	Private	☐
Other	☐	Poor Roads	☐	Very Noisy	☐	No Privacy	☐

Safety:

Felt Very Safe ☐   Moderately Safe ☐   Felt Unsafe ☐

Wi-Fi:

Wi-Fi Available	☐
Poor Signal	☐
Good Signal	☐
Excellent Signal	☐
Notes:	

Notes:

_____
_____
_____
_____
_____
_____

Who Was With Us? _____

_____

_____

People We Met: _____

_____

_____

Fun Things We Did: _____

_____

_____

Things to Remember For Next Time: _____

_____

_____

_____

_____

Favorite Memories: _____

_____

_____

_____

_____

_____

_____

All About The Scenery: _____

_____

_____

_____

_____

_____

Area Around The Campground:

What Was the Weather Like? _____
_____
_____

Sightseeing/Activities:	Distance:	Fees/Contact Info:
_____	_____	_____
_____	_____	_____
_____	_____	_____
_____	_____	_____
_____	_____	_____

Nearby Restaurants: _____
_____
_____

Nearby Groceries: _____
_____
_____

Overall Thoughts About This Campground (Do you want
to revisit? Site # You Want to Reserve? Important Things
To Remember, etc.)

_____
_____
_____
_____
_____
_____
_____

Notes, Lists, Drawings, Photos

Dates: _____ to _____

Campground: _____

Traveled From: _____ Miles: _____ Time: _____

Fees: _____ Pull-Through ☐ Back-In ☐

Hookups:

FHU	☐	W/E Only	☐
50 & 30 Amp	☐	30 Amp Only	☐
Dry Camp	☐	Dumping	☐
Notes:			

Restrooms/Showers:

Flush Toilets	Yes ☐	No ☐	
Showers Yes ☐ No ☐	Free ☐ Paid ☐		
Enough Hot Water Yes ☐	No ☐		
Cleanliness:			

Amenities:

Pool	☐	Hot Tub	☐	Game Room	☐	Laundry	☐
Restaurant	☐	Pet-Friendly	☐	Dog Park	☐	Playground	☐
Shuffleboard	☐	Hiking	☐	Boating	☐	Fishing	☐
Horses	☐	Fitness Room	☐	Store	☐	Ice	☐
Firewood	☐		☐		☐		☐
Notes:							

Site Details for Site # _____:

RV Pad		Size/Access		Shade/Noise		Picnic Area	
Level	☐	Small	☐	No Shade	☐	Fire Ring	☐
Not Level	☐	Medium	☐	Partial Shade	☐	Fires Allowed	☐
Paved	☐	Large	☐	Full Shade	☐	Picnic Table	☐
Grass	☐	Tight Turns	☐	Quiet	☐	Good View	☐
Dirt	☐	Low Trees	☐	Light Noise	☐	Private	☐
Other	☐	Poor Roads	☐	Very Noisy	☐	No Privacy	☐

Safety:

Felt Very Safe ☐   Moderately Safe ☐   Felt Unsafe ☐

Wi-Fi:

Wi-Fi Available	☐
Poor Signal	☐
Good Signal	☐
Excellent Signal	☐
Notes:	

Notes:

_____
_____
_____
_____
_____
_____
_____

Who Was With Us? _____

_____

_____

People We Met: _____

_____

_____

Fun Things We Did: _____

_____

_____

Things to Remember For Next Time: _____

_____

_____

_____

_____

Favorite Memories: _____

_____

_____

_____

_____

_____

_____

All About The Scenery: _____

_____

_____

_____

_____

_____

Area Around The Campground:

What Was the Weather Like? _____
_____
_____

Sightseeing/Activities:	Distance:	Fees/Contact Info:
_____	_____	_____
_____	_____	_____
_____	_____	_____
_____	_____	_____
_____	_____	_____

Nearby Restaurants: _____
_____
_____

Nearby Groceries: _____
_____
_____

Overall Thoughts About This Campground (Do you want to revisit? Site # You Want to Reserve? Important Things To Remember, etc.)

_____
_____
_____
_____
_____
_____
_____

Notes, Lists, Drawings, Photos

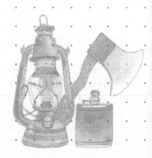

Dates: _____ **to** _____

Campground: _____

Traveled From: _____ **Miles:** _____ **Time:** _____

Fees: _____ **Pull-Through** ☐ **Back-In** ☐

Hookups:

FHU	☐	W/E Only	☐
50 & 30 Amp	☐	30 Amp Only	☐
Dry Camp	☐	Dumping	☐
Notes:			

Restrooms/Showers:

Flush Toilets		Yes ☐		No ☐	
Showers Yes ☐	No ☐	Free ☐	Paid ☐		
Enough Hot Water	Yes ☐	No ☐			
Cleanliness:					

Amenities:

Pool	☐	Hot Tub	☐	Game Room	☐	Laundry	☐
Restaurant	☐	Pet-Friendly	☐	Dog Park	☐	Playground	☐
Shuffleboard	☐	Hiking	☐	Boating	☐	Fishing	☐
Horses	☐	Fitness Room	☐	Store	☐	Ice	☐
Firewood	☐		☐		☐		☐
Notes:							

Site Details for Site # _____:

RV Pad		Size/Access		Shade/Noise		Picnic Area	
Level	☐	Small	☐	No Shade	☐	Fire Ring	☐
Not Level	☐	Medium	☐	Partial Shade	☐	Fires Allowed	☐
Paved	☐	Large	☐	Full Shade	☐	Picnic Table	☐
Grass	☐	Tight Turns	☐	Quiet	☐	Good View	☐
Dirt	☐	Low Trees	☐	Light Noise	☐	Private	☐
Other	☐	Poor Roads	☐	Very Noisy	☐	No Privacy	☐

Safety:

Felt Very Safe ☐   Moderately Safe ☐   Felt Unsafe ☐

Wi-Fi:

Wi-Fi Available	☐
Poor Signal	☐
Good Signal	☐
Excellent Signal	☐
Notes:	

Notes:

_____
_____
_____
_____
_____
_____
_____

Who Was With Us? _____
_____
_____

People We Met: _____
_____
_____

Fun Things We Did: _____
_____
_____

Things to Remember For Next Time: _____
_____
_____
_____
_____

Favorite Memories: _____
_____
_____
_____
_____
_____
_____
_____

All About The Scenery: _____
_____
_____
_____
_____
_____

Area Around The Campground:

What Was the Weather Like? _____
_____
_____

Sightseeing/Activities:	Distance:	Fees/Contact Info:
_____	_____	_____
_____	_____	_____
_____	_____	_____
_____	_____	_____
_____	_____	_____

Nearby Restaurants: _____
_____
_____

Nearby Groceries: _____
_____
_____

Overall Thoughts About This Campground (Do you want
to revisit? Site # You Want to Reserve? Important Things
To Remember, etc.)

_____
_____
_____
_____
_____
_____
_____

Notes, Lists, Drawings, Photos

Trip #10

Dates: _____ to _____

Campground: _____

Traveled From: _____ Miles: _____ Time: _____

Fees: _____ Pull-Through ☐ Back-In ☐

Hookups:

FHU	☐	W/E Only	☐
50 & 30 Amp	☐	30 Amp Only	☐
Dry Camp	☐	Dumping	☐
Notes:			

Restrooms/Showers:

Flush Toilets	Yes ☐	No ☐	
Showers Yes ☐	No ☐	Free ☐	Paid ☐
Enough Hot Water	Yes ☐	No ☐	
Cleanliness:			

Amenities:

Pool	☐	Hot Tub	☐	Game Room	☐	Laundry	☐
Restaurant	☐	Pet-Friendly	☐	Dog Park	☐	Playground	☐
Shuffleboard	☐	Hiking	☐	Boating	☐	Fishing	☐
Horses	☐	Fitness Room	☐	Store	☐	Ice	☐
Firewood	☐		☐		☐		☐
Notes:							

Site Details for Site # _____:

RV Pad		Size/Access		Shade/Noise		Picnic Area	
Level	☐	Small	☐	No Shade	☐	Fire Ring	☐
Not Level	☐	Medium	☐	Partial Shade	☐	Fires Allowed	☐
Paved	☐	Large	☐	Full Shade	☐	Picnic Table	☐
Grass	☐	Tight Turns	☐	Quiet	☐	Good View	☐
Dirt	☐	Low Trees	☐	Light Noise	☐	Private	☐
Other	☐	Poor Roads	☐	Very Noisy	☐	No Privacy	☐

Safety:

Felt Very Safe ☐   Moderately Safe ☐   Felt Unsafe ☐

Wi-Fi:

Wi-Fi Available	☐
Poor Signal	☐
Good Signal	☐
Excellent Signal	☐
Notes:	

Notes:

_____
_____
_____
_____
_____
_____

Who Was With Us? _____

_____

_____

People We Met: _____

_____

_____

Fun Things We Did: _____

_____

_____

Things to Remember For Next Time: _____

_____

_____

_____

_____

Favorite Memories: _____

_____

_____

_____

_____

_____

_____

_____

All About The Scenery: _____

_____

_____

_____

_____

_____

Area Around The Campground:

What Was the Weather Like? _____
_____
_____

Sightseeing/Activities:	Distance:	Fees/Contact Info:
_____	_____	_____
_____	_____	_____
_____	_____	_____
_____	_____	_____
_____	_____	_____

Nearby Restaurants: _____
_____
_____

Nearby Groceries: _____
_____
_____

Overall Thoughts About This Campground (Do you want
to revisit? Site # You Want to Reserve? Important Things
To Remember, etc.)

_____
_____
_____
_____
_____
_____
_____

Notes, Lists, Drawings, Photos

Dates: _____ to _____

Campground: _____

Traveled From: _____ Miles: _____ Time: _____

Fees: _____ Pull-Through ☐ Back-In ☐

Hookups:

FHU	☐	W/E Only	☐
50 & 30 Amp	☐	30 Amp Only	☐
Dry Camp	☐	Dumping	☐
Notes:			

Restrooms/Showers:

Flush Toilets Yes ☐ No ☐	
Showers Yes ☐ No ☐ Free ☐ Paid ☐	
Enough Hot Water Yes ☐ No ☐	
Cleanliness:	

Amenities:

Pool	☐	Hot Tub	☐	Game Room	☐	Laundry	☐
Restaurant	☐	Pet-Friendly	☐	Dog Park	☐	Playground	☐
Shuffleboard	☐	Hiking	☐	Boating	☐	Fishing	☐
Horses	☐	Fitness Room	☐	Store	☐	Ice	☐
Firewood	☐		☐		☐		☐
Notes:							

Site Details for Site # _____:

RV Pad		Size/Access		Shade/Noise		Picnic Area	
Level	☐	Small	☐	No Shade	☐	Fire Ring	☐
Not Level	☐	Medium	☐	Partial Shade	☐	Fires Allowed	☐
Paved	☐	Large	☐	Full Shade	☐	Picnic Table	☐
Grass	☐	Tight Turns	☐	Quiet	☐	Good View	☐
Dirt	☐	Low Trees	☐	Light Noise	☐	Private	☐
Other	☐	Poor Roads	☐	Very Noisy	☐	No Privacy	☐

Safety:

Felt Very Safe ☐   Moderately Safe ☐   Felt Unsafe ☐

Wi-Fi:

Wi-Fi Available	☐
Poor Signal	☐
Good Signal	☐
Excellent Signal	☐
Notes:	

Notes:

_____
_____
_____
_____
_____
_____
_____

Who Was With Us? _____
_____
_____

People We Met: _____
_____
_____

Fun Things We Did: _____
_____
_____

Things to Remember For Next Time: _____
_____
_____
_____
_____

Favorite Memories: _____
_____
_____
_____
_____
_____
_____
_____

All About The Scenery: _____
_____
_____
_____
_____
_____

Area Around The Campground:

What Was the Weather Like? _____
_____
_____

Sightseeing/Activities:	Distance:	Fees/Contact Info:
_____	_____	_____
_____	_____	_____
_____	_____	_____
_____	_____	_____
_____	_____	_____

Nearby Restaurants: _____
_____
_____

Nearby Groceries: _____
_____
_____

Overall Thoughts About This Campground (Do you want to revisit? Site # You Want to Reserve? Important Things To Remember, etc.)

_____
_____
_____
_____
_____
_____
_____

Notes, Lists, Drawings, Photos

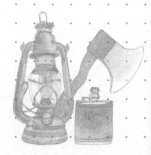

Dates: _____ **to** _____

Campground: _____

Traveled From: _____ **Miles:** ____ **Time:** ____

Fees: _____ **Pull-Through** ☐ **Back-In** ☐

Hookups:

FHU	☐	W/E Only	☐
50 & 30 Amp	☐	30 Amp Only	☐
Dry Camp	☐	Dumping	☐
Notes:			

Restrooms/Showers:

Flush Toilets	Yes ☐	No ☐		
Showers	Yes ☐	No ☐	Free ☐	Paid ☐
Enough Hot Water	Yes ☐	No ☐		
Cleanliness:				

Amenities:

Pool	☐	Hot Tub	☐	Game Room	☐	Laundry	☐
Restaurant	☐	Pet-Friendly	☐	Dog Park	☐	Playground	☐
Shuffleboard	☐	Hiking	☐	Boating	☐	Fishing	☐
Horses	☐	Fitness Room	☐	Store	☐	Ice	☐
Firewood	☐		☐		☐		☐
Notes:							

Site Details for Site # ____:

RV Pad		Size/Access		Shade/Noise		Picnic Area	
Level	☐	Small	☐	No Shade	☐	Fire Ring	☐
Not Level	☐	Medium	☐	Partial Shade	☐	Fires Allowed	☐
Paved	☐	Large	☐	Full Shade	☐	Picnic Table	☐
Grass	☐	Tight Turns	☐	Quiet	☐	Good View	☐
Dirt	☐	Low Trees	☐	Light Noise	☐	Private	☐
Other	☐	Poor Roads	☐	Very Noisy	☐	No Privacy	☐

Safety:

Felt Very Safe ☐   Moderately Safe ☐   Felt Unsafe ☐

Wi-Fi:

Wi-Fi Available	☐
Poor Signal	☐
Good Signal	☐
Excellent Signal	☐
Notes:	

Notes:

_____
_____
_____
_____
_____
_____
_____

Who Was With Us? _____
_____
_____

People We Met: _____
_____
_____

Fun Things We Did: _____
_____
_____

Things to Remember For Next Time: _____
_____
_____
_____
_____

Favorite Memories: _____
_____
_____
_____
_____
_____
_____

All About The Scenery: _____
_____
_____
_____
_____
_____

Area Around The Campground:

What Was the Weather Like? _____
_____
_____

Sightseeing/Activities:	Distance:	Fees/Contact Info:
_____	_____	_____
_____	_____	_____
_____	_____	_____
_____	_____	_____
_____	_____	_____

Nearby Restaurants: _____
_____
_____

Nearby Groceries: _____
_____
_____

Overall Thoughts About This Campground (Do you want
to revisit? Site # You Want to Reserve? Important Things
To Remember, etc.)

_____
_____
_____
_____
_____
_____
_____

Notes, Lists, Drawings, Photos

Trip #13

Dates: _____ to _____

Campground: _____

Traveled From: _____ Miles: _____ Time: _____

Fees: _____ Pull-Through ☐ Back-In ☐

Hookups:

FHU	☐	W/E Only	☐
50 & 30 Amp	☐	30 Amp Only	☐
Dry Camp	☐	Dumping	☐
Notes:			

Restrooms/Showers:

Flush Toilets Yes ☐ No ☐	
Showers Yes ☐ No ☐ Free ☐ Paid ☐	
Enough Hot Water Yes ☐ No ☐	
Cleanliness:	

Amenities:

Pool	☐	Hot Tub	☐	Game Room	☐	Laundry	☐
Restaurant	☐	Pet-Friendly	☐	Dog Park	☐	Playground	☐
Shuffleboard	☐	Hiking	☐	Boating	☐	Fishing	☐
Horses	☐	Fitness Room	☐	Store	☐	Ice	☐
Firewood	☐		☐		☐		☐
Notes:							

Site Details for Site # _____:

RV Pad		Size/Access		Shade/Noise		Picnic Area	
Level	☐	Small	☐	No Shade	☐	Fire Ring	☐
Not Level	☐	Medium	☐	Partial Shade	☐	Fires Allowed	☐
Paved	☐	Large	☐	Full Shade	☐	Picnic Table	☐
Grass	☐	Tight Turns	☐	Quiet	☐	Good View	☐
Dirt	☐	Low Trees	☐	Light Noise	☐	Private	☐
Other	☐	Poor Roads	☐	Very Noisy	☐	No Privacy	☐

Safety:

Felt Very Safe ☐   Moderately Safe ☐   Felt Unsafe ☐

Wi-Fi:

Wi-Fi Available	☐
Poor Signal	☐
Good Signal	☐
Excellent Signal	☐
Notes:	

Notes:

_____
_____
_____
_____
_____
_____
_____
_____
_____

Who Was With Us? _____
_____
_____

People We Met: _____
_____
_____

Fun Things We Did: _____
_____
_____

Things to Remember For Next Time: _____
_____
_____
_____
_____

Favorite Memories: _____
_____
_____
_____
_____
_____
_____

All About The Scenery: _____
_____
_____
_____
_____
_____

Area Around The Campground:

What Was the Weather Like? _____
_____
_____

Sightseeing/Activities:	Distance:	Fees/Contact Info:
_____	_____	_____
_____	_____	_____
_____	_____	_____
_____	_____	_____
_____	_____	_____

Nearby Restaurants: _____
_____
_____

Nearby Groceries: _____
_____
_____

Overall Thoughts About This Campground (Do you want
to revisit? Site # You Want to Reserve? Important Things
To Remember, etc.)

_____
_____
_____
_____
_____
_____
_____

Notes, Lists, Drawings, Photos

Dates: _____ **to** _____

Campground: _____

Traveled From: _____ **Miles:** _____ **Time:** _____

Fees: _____ **Pull-Through** ☐ **Back-In** ☐

Hookups:

FHU	☐	W/E Only	☐
50 & 30 Amp	☐	30 Amp Only	☐
Dry Camp	☐	Dumping	☐
Notes:			

Restrooms/Showers:

Flush Toilets	Yes ☐	No ☐
Showers Yes ☐ No ☐	Free ☐	Paid ☐
Enough Hot Water Yes ☐	No ☐	
Cleanliness:		

Amenities:

Pool	☐	Hot Tub	☐	Game Room	☐	Laundry	☐
Restaurant	☐	Pet-Friendly	☐	Dog Park	☐	Playground	☐
Shuffleboard	☐	Hiking	☐	Boating	☐	Fishing	☐
Horses	☐	Fitness Room	☐	Store	☐	Ice	☐
Firewood	☐		☐		☐		☐
Notes:							

Site Details for Site # ____:

RV Pad		Size/Access		Shade/Noise		Picnic Area	
Level	☐	Small	☐	No Shade	☐	Fire Ring	☐
Not Level	☐	Medium	☐	Partial Shade	☐	Fires Allowed	☐
Paved	☐	Large	☐	Full Shade	☐	Picnic Table	☐
Grass	☐	Tight Turns	☐	Quiet	☐	Good View	☐
Dirt	☐	Low Trees	☐	Light Noise	☐	Private	☐
Other	☐	Poor Roads	☐	Very Noisy	☐	No Privacy	☐

Safety:

Felt Very Safe ☐   Moderately Safe ☐   Felt Unsafe ☐

Wi-Fi:

Wi-Fi Available	☐
Poor Signal	☐
Good Signal	☐
Excellent Signal	☐
Notes:	

Notes:

_____

_____

_____

_____

_____

_____

_____

_____

Who Was With Us? _____
_____
_____

People We Met: _____
_____
_____

Fun Things We Did: _____
_____
_____

Things to Remember For Next Time: _____
_____
_____
_____
_____

Favorite Memories: _____
_____
_____
_____
_____
_____
_____

All About The Scenery: _____
_____
_____
_____
_____
_____

Area Around The Campground:

What Was the Weather Like? _____
_____
_____

Sightseeing/Activities:	Distance:	Fees/Contact Info:
_____	_____	_____
_____	_____	_____
_____	_____	_____
_____	_____	_____
_____	_____	_____

Nearby Restaurants: _____
_____
_____

Nearby Groceries: _____
_____
_____

Overall Thoughts About This Campground (Do you want
to revisit? Site # You Want to Reserve? Important Things
To Remember, etc.)

_____
_____
_____
_____
_____
_____
_____

Notes, Lists, Drawings, Photos

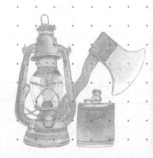

Dates: _____ **to** _____

Campground: _____

Traveled From: _____ **Miles:** _____ **Time:** _____

Fees: _____**Pull-Through** ☐ **Back-In** ☐

Hookups:

FHU	☐	W/E Only	☐
50 & 30 Amp	☐	30 Amp Only	☐
Dry Camp	☐	Dumping	☐
Notes:			

Restrooms/Showers:

Flush Toilets Yes ☐ No ☐	
Showers Yes ☐ No ☐ Free ☐ Paid ☐	
Enough Hot Water Yes ☐ No ☐	
Cleanliness:	

Amenities:

Pool	☐	Hot Tub	☐	Game Room	☐	Laundry	☐
Restaurant	☐	Pet-Friendly	☐	Dog Park	☐	Playground	☐
Shuffleboard	☐	Hiking	☐	Boating	☐	Fishing	☐
Horses	☐	Fitness Room	☐	Store	☐	Ice	☐
Firewood	☐		☐		☐		☐
Notes:							

Site Details for Site # ____:

RV Pad		Size/Access		Shade/Noise		Picnic Area	
Level	☐	Small	☐	No Shade	☐	Fire Ring	☐
Not Level	☐	Medium	☐	Partial Shade	☐	Fires Allowed	☐
Paved	☐	Large	☐	Full Shade	☐	Picnic Table	☐
Grass	☐	Tight Turns	☐	Quiet	☐	Good View	☐
Dirt	☐	Low Trees	☐	Light Noise	☐	Private	☐
Other	☐	Poor Roads	☐	Very Noisy	☐	No Privacy	☐

Safety:

Felt Very Safe ☐   Moderately Safe ☐   Felt Unsafe ☐

Wi-Fi:

Wi-Fi Available	☐
Poor Signal	☐
Good Signal	☐
Excellent Signal	☐
Notes:	

Notes:

_____
_____
_____
_____
_____
_____
_____

Who Was With Us? _____
_____
_____

People We Met: _____
_____
_____

Fun Things We Did: _____
_____
_____

Things to Remember For Next Time: _____
_____
_____
_____
_____

Favorite Memories: _____
_____
_____
_____
_____
_____
_____
_____

All About The Scenery: _____
_____
_____
_____
_____
_____

Area Around The Campground:

What Was the Weather Like? _____

_____

_____

Sightseeing/Activities:	Distance:	Fees/Contact Info:
_____	_____	_____
_____	_____	_____
_____	_____	_____
_____	_____	_____
_____	_____	_____

Nearby Restaurants: _____

_____

_____

Nearby Groceries: _____

_____

_____

Overall Thoughts About This Campground (Do you want to revisit? Site # You Want to Reserve? Important Things To Remember, etc.)

_____

_____

_____

_____

_____

_____

_____

_____

Notes, Lists, Drawings, Photos

Dates: _____ **to** _____

Campground: _____

Traveled From: _____ **Miles:** _____ **Time:** _____

Fees: _____ **Pull-Through** ☐ **Back-In** ☐

Hookups:

FHU	☐	W/E Only	☐
50 & 30 Amp	☐	30 Amp Only	☐
Dry Camp	☐	Dumping	☐
Notes:			

Restrooms/Showers:

Flush Toilets		Yes ☐		No ☐	
Showers Yes ☐	No ☐	Free ☐	Paid ☐		
Enough Hot Water	Yes ☐		No ☐		
Cleanliness:					

Amenities:

Pool	☐	Hot Tub	☐	Game Room	☐	Laundry	☐
Restaurant	☐	Pet-Friendly	☐	Dog Park	☐	Playground	☐
Shuffleboard	☐	Hiking	☐	Boating	☐	Fishing	☐
Horses	☐	Fitness Room	☐	Store	☐	Ice	☐
Firewood	☐		☐		☐		☐
Notes:							

Site Details for Site # _____:

RV Pad		Size/Access		Shade/Noise		Picnic Area	
Level	☐	Small	☐	No Shade	☐	Fire Ring	☐
Not Level	☐	Medium	☐	Partial Shade	☐	Fires Allowed	☐
Paved	☐	Large	☐	Full Shade	☐	Picnic Table	☐
Grass	☐	Tight Turns	☐	Quiet	☐	Good View	☐
Dirt	☐	Low Trees	☐	Light Noise	☐	Private	☐
Other	☐	Poor Roads	☐	Very Noisy	☐	No Privacy	☐

Safety:

Felt Very Safe ☐   Moderately Safe ☐   Felt Unsafe ☐

Wi-Fi:

Wi-Fi Available	☐
Poor Signal	☐
Good Signal	☐
Excellent Signal	☐
Notes:	

Notes:

_____
_____
_____
_____
_____
_____
_____

Who Was With Us?_____

_____

_____

People We Met: _____

_____

_____

Fun Things We Did: _____

_____

_____

Things to Remember For Next Time: _____

_____

_____

_____

_____

Favorite Memories: _____

_____

_____

_____

_____

_____

_____

All About The Scenery: _____

_____

_____

_____

_____

_____

Area Around The Campground:

What Was the Weather Like? _____

_____

_____

Sightseeing/Activities:	Distance:	Fees/Contact Info:
_____	_____	_____
_____	_____	_____
_____	_____	_____
_____	_____	_____
_____	_____	_____

Nearby Restaurants: _____

_____

_____

Nearby Groceries: _____

_____

_____

Overall Thoughts About This Campground (Do you want
to revisit? Site # You Want to Reserve? Important Things
To Remember, etc.)

_____

_____

_____

_____

_____

_____

_____

Notes, Lists, Drawings, Photos

Dates: _____ **to** _____

Campground: _____

Traveled From: _____**Miles:** _____ **Time:** _____

Fees: _____**Pull-Through** ☐ **Back-In** ☐

Hookups:

FHU	☐	W/E Only	☐
50 & 30 Amp	☐	30 Amp Only	☐
Dry Camp	☐	Dumping	☐
Notes:			

Restrooms/Showers:

Flush Toilets Yes ☐ No ☐	
Showers Yes ☐ No ☐ Free ☐ Paid ☐	
Enough Hot Water Yes ☐ No ☐	
Cleanliness:	

Amenities:

Pool	☐	Hot Tub	☐	Game Room	☐	Laundry	☐
Restaurant	☐	Pet-Friendly	☐	Dog Park	☐	Playground	☐
Shuffleboard	☐	Hiking	☐	Boating	☐	Fishing	☐
Horses	☐	Fitness Room	☐	Store	☐	Ice	☐
Firewood	☐		☐		☐		☐
Notes:							

Site Details for Site # _____:

RV Pad		Size/Access		Shade/Noise		Picnic Area	
Level	☐	Small	☐	No Shade	☐	Fire Ring	☐
Not Level	☐	Medium	☐	Partial Shade	☐	Fires Allowed	☐
Paved	☐	Large	☐	Full Shade	☐	Picnic Table	☐
Grass	☐	Tight Turns	☐	Quiet	☐	Good View	☐
Dirt	☐	Low Trees	☐	Light Noise	☐	Private	☐
Other	☐	Poor Roads	☐	Very Noisy	☐	No Privacy	☐

Safety:

Felt Very Safe ☐   Moderately Safe ☐   Felt Unsafe ☐

Wi-Fi:

Wi-Fi Available	☐
Poor Signal	☐
Good Signal	☐
Excellent Signal	☐
Notes:	

Notes:

_____

_____

_____

_____

_____

_____

_____

Who Was With Us? _____
_____
_____

People We Met: _____
_____
_____

Fun Things We Did: _____
_____
_____

Things to Remember For Next Time: _____
_____
_____
_____
_____

Favorite Memories: _____
_____
_____
_____
_____
_____
_____
_____

All About The Scenery: _____
_____
_____
_____
_____
_____

Area Around The Campground:

What Was the Weather Like? _____
_____
_____

Sightseeing/Activities:	Distance:	Fees/Contact Info:
_____	_____	_____
_____	_____	_____
_____	_____	_____
_____	_____	_____
_____	_____	_____

Nearby Restaurants: _____
_____
_____

Nearby Groceries: _____
_____
_____

Overall Thoughts About This Campground (Do you want
to revisit? Site # You Want to Reserve? Important Things
To Remember, etc.)

_____
_____
_____
_____
_____
_____
_____
_____

Notes, Lists, Drawings, Photos

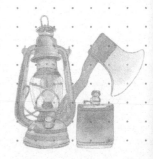

Dates: _____ to _____

Campground: _____

Traveled From: _____ Miles: _____ Time: _____

Fees: _____ Pull-Through ☐ Back-In ☐

Hookups:

FHU	☐	W/E Only	☐
50 & 30 Amp	☐	30 Amp Only	☐
Dry Camp	☐	Dumping	☐
Notes:			

Restrooms/Showers:

Flush Toilets	Yes ☐	No ☐
Showers Yes ☐ No ☐	Free ☐	Paid ☐
Enough Hot Water Yes ☐	No ☐	
Cleanliness:		

Amenities:

Pool	☐	Hot Tub	☐	Game Room	☐	Laundry	☐
Restaurant	☐	Pet-Friendly	☐	Dog Park	☐	Playground	☐
Shuffleboard	☐	Hiking	☐	Boating	☐	Fishing	☐
Horses	☐	Fitness Room	☐	Store	☐	Ice	☐
Firewood	☐		☐		☐		☐
Notes:							

Site Details for Site # _____:

RV Pad		Size/Access		Shade/Noise		Picnic Area	
Level	☐	Small	☐	No Shade	☐	Fire Ring	☐
Not Level	☐	Medium	☐	Partial Shade	☐	Fires Allowed	☐
Paved	☐	Large	☐	Full Shade	☐	Picnic Table	☐
Grass	☐	Tight Turns	☐	Quiet	☐	Good View	☐
Dirt	☐	Low Trees	☐	Light Noise	☐	Private	☐
Other	☐	Poor Roads	☐	Very Noisy	☐	No Privacy	☐

Safety:

Felt Very Safe ☐   Moderately Safe ☐   Felt Unsafe ☐

Wi-Fi:

Wi-Fi Available	☐
Poor Signal	☐
Good Signal	☐
Excellent Signal	☐
Notes:	

Notes:

_____
_____
_____
_____
_____
_____
_____

Who Was With Us? _____
_____
_____

People We Met: _____
_____
_____

Fun Things We Did: _____
_____
_____

Things to Remember For Next Time: _____
_____
_____
_____
_____

Favorite Memories: _____
_____
_____
_____
_____
_____
_____
_____

All About The Scenery: _____
_____
_____
_____
_____
_____

Area Around The Campground:

What Was the Weather Like? _____
_____
_____

Sightseeing/Activities:	Distance:	Fees/Contact Info:
_____	_____	_____
_____	_____	_____
_____	_____	_____
_____	_____	_____
_____	_____	_____

Nearby Restaurants: _____
_____
_____

Nearby Groceries: _____
_____
_____

Overall Thoughts About This Campground (Do you want
to revisit? Site # You Want to Reserve? Important Things
To Remember, etc.)

_____
_____
_____
_____
_____
_____
_____
_____

Notes, Lists, Drawings, Photos

Dates: _____ to _____

Campground: _____

Traveled From: _____ Miles: _____ Time: _____

Fees: _____ Pull-Through ☐ Back-In ☐

Hookups:

FHU	☐	W/E Only	☐
50 & 30 Amp	☐	30 Amp Only	☐
Dry Camp	☐	Dumping	☐
Notes:			

Restrooms/Showers:

Flush Toilets	Yes ☐ No ☐
Showers Yes ☐ No ☐	Free ☐ Paid ☐
Enough Hot Water	Yes ☐ No ☐
Cleanliness:	

Amenities:

Pool	☐	Hot Tub	☐	Game Room	☐	Laundry	☐
Restaurant	☐	Pet-Friendly	☐	Dog Park	☐	Playground	☐
Shuffleboard	☐	Hiking	☐	Boating	☐	Fishing	☐
Horses	☐	Fitness Room	☐	Store	☐	Ice	☐
Firewood	☐		☐		☐		☐
Notes:							

Site Details for Site # _____:

RV Pad		Size/Access		Shade/Noise		Picnic Area	
Level	☐	Small	☐	No Shade	☐	Fire Ring	☐
Not Level	☐	Medium	☐	Partial Shade	☐	Fires Allowed	☐
Paved	☐	Large	☐	Full Shade	☐	Picnic Table	☐
Grass	☐	Tight Turns	☐	Quiet	☐	Good View	☐
Dirt	☐	Low Trees	☐	Light Noise	☐	Private	☐
Other	☐	Poor Roads	☐	Very Noisy	☐	No Privacy	☐

Safety:

Felt Very Safe ☐   Moderately Safe ☐   Felt Unsafe ☐

Wi-Fi:

Wi-Fi Available	☐
Poor Signal	☐
Good Signal	☐
Excellent Signal	☐
Notes:	

Notes:

_____
_____
_____
_____
_____
_____
_____
_____

Who Was With Us? _____

_____

_____

People We Met: _____

_____

_____

Fun Things We Did: _____

_____

_____

Things to Remember For Next Time: _____

_____

_____

_____

_____

Favorite Memories: _____

_____

_____

_____

_____

_____

_____

_____

All About The Scenery: _____

_____

_____

_____

_____

_____

Area Around The Campground:

What Was the Weather Like? _____

_____

_____

Sightseeing/Activities:	Distance:	Fees/Contact Info:
_____	_____	_____
_____	_____	_____
_____	_____	_____
_____	_____	_____
_____	_____	_____

Nearby Restaurants: _____

_____

_____

Nearby Groceries: _____

_____

_____

Overall Thoughts About This Campground (Do you want
to revisit? Site # You Want to Reserve? Important Things
To Remember, etc.)

_____

_____

_____

_____

_____

_____

_____

Notes, Lists, Drawings, Photos

Dates: _____ **to** _____

Campground: _____

Traveled From: _____ **Miles:** _____ **Time:** _____

Fees: _____ Pull-Through ☐ Back-In ☐

Hookups:

FHU	☐	W/E Only	☐
50 & 30 Amp	☐	30 Amp Only	☐
Dry Camp	☐	Dumping	☐
Notes:			

Restrooms/Showers:

Flush Toilets Yes ☐ No ☐
Showers Yes ☐ No ☐ Free ☐ Paid ☐
Enough Hot Water Yes ☐ No ☐
Cleanliness:

Amenities:

Pool	☐	Hot Tub	☐	Game Room	☐	Laundry	☐
Restaurant	☐	Pet-Friendly	☐	Dog Park	☐	Playground	☐
Shuffleboard	☐	Hiking	☐	Boating	☐	Fishing	☐
Horses	☐	Fitness Room	☐	Store	☐	Ice	☐
Firewood	☐		☐		☐		☐
Notes:							

Site Details for Site # _____:

RV Pad		Size/Access		Shade/Noise		Picnic Area	
Level	☐	Small	☐	No Shade	☐	Fire Ring	☐
Not Level	☐	Medium	☐	Partial Shade	☐	Fires Allowed	☐
Paved	☐	Large	☐	Full Shade	☐	Picnic Table	☐
Grass	☐	Tight Turns	☐	Quiet	☐	Good View	☐
Dirt	☐	Low Trees	☐	Light Noise	☐	Private	☐
Other	☐	Poor Roads	☐	Very Noisy	☐	No Privacy	☐

Safety:

Felt Very Safe ☐   Moderately Safe ☐   Felt Unsafe ☐

Wi-Fi:

Wi-Fi Available	☐
Poor Signal	☐
Good Signal	☐
Excellent Signal	☐
Notes:	

Notes:

_____
_____
_____
_____
_____
_____
_____

Who Was With Us? _____
_____
_____

People We Met: _____
_____
_____

Fun Things We Did: _____
_____
_____

Things to Remember For Next Time: _____
_____
_____
_____
_____

Favorite Memories: _____
_____
_____
_____
_____
_____
_____
_____

All About The Scenery: _____
_____
_____
_____
_____
_____

Area Around The Campground:

What Was the Weather Like? _____
_____
_____

Sightseeing/Activities:	Distance:	Fees/Contact Info:
_____	_____	_____
_____	_____	_____
_____	_____	_____
_____	_____	_____
_____	_____	_____

Nearby Restaurants: _____
_____
_____

Nearby Groceries: _____
_____
_____

Overall Thoughts About This Campground (Do you want
to revisit? Site # You Want to Reserve? Important Things
To Remember, etc.)

_____
_____
_____
_____
_____
_____
_____

Notes, Lists, Drawings, Photos

Trip #21

Dates: _____ **to** _____

Campground: _____

Traveled From: _____ **Miles:** _____ **Time:** _____

Fees: _____ **Pull-Through** ☐ **Back-In** ☐

Hookups:

FHU	☐	W/E Only	☐
50 & 30 Amp	☐	30 Amp Only	☐
Dry Camp	☐	Dumping	☐
Notes:			

Restrooms/Showers:

Flush Toilets		Yes ☐		No ☐
Showers Yes ☐	No ☐		Free ☐	Paid ☐
Enough Hot Water		Yes ☐		No ☐
Cleanliness:				

Amenities:

Pool	☐	Hot Tub	☐	Game Room	☐	Laundry	☐
Restaurant	☐	Pet-Friendly	☐	Dog Park	☐	Playground	☐
Shuffleboard	☐	Hiking	☐	Boating	☐	Fishing	☐
Horses	☐	Fitness Room	☐	Store	☐	Ice	☐
Firewood	☐		☐		☐		☐
Notes:							

Site Details for Site # _____:

RV Pad		Size/Access		Shade/Noise		Picnic Area	
Level	☐	Small	☐	No Shade	☐	Fire Ring	☐
Not Level	☐	Medium	☐	Partial Shade	☐	Fires Allowed	☐
Paved	☐	Large	☐	Full Shade	☐	Picnic Table	☐
Grass	☐	Tight Turns	☐	Quiet	☐	Good View	☐
Dirt	☐	Low Trees	☐	Light Noise	☐	Private	☐
Other	☐	Poor Roads	☐	Very Noisy	☐	No Privacy	☐

Safety:

Felt Very Safe ☐   Moderately Safe ☐   Felt Unsafe ☐

Wi-Fi:

Wi-Fi Available	☐
Poor Signal	☐
Good Signal	☐
Excellent Signal	☐
Notes:	

Notes:

_____
_____
_____
_____
_____
_____
_____

Who Was With Us? _____

_____

_____

People We Met: _____

_____

_____

Fun Things We Did: _____

_____

_____

Things to Remember For Next Time: _____

_____

_____

_____

_____

Favorite Memories: _____

_____

_____

_____

_____

_____

_____

All About The Scenery: _____

_____

_____

_____

_____

_____

Area Around The Campground:

What Was the Weather Like? _____
_____
_____

Sightseeing/Activities:	Distance:	Fees/Contact Info:
_____	_____	_____
_____	_____	_____
_____	_____	_____
_____	_____	_____
_____	_____	_____

Nearby Restaurants: _____
_____
_____

Nearby Groceries: _____
_____
_____

Overall Thoughts About This Campground (Do you want
to revisit? Site # You Want to Reserve? Important Things
To Remember, etc.)

_____
_____
_____
_____
_____
_____
_____
_____

Notes, Lists, Drawings, Photos

Dates: _____ to _____

Campground: _____

Traveled From: _____ Miles: _____ Time: _____

Fees: _____ Pull-Through ☐ Back-In ☐

Hookups:

FHU	☐	W/E Only	☐
50 & 30 Amp	☐	30 Amp Only	☐
Dry Camp	☐	Dumping	☐
Notes:			

Restrooms/Showers:

Flush Toilets Yes ☐ No ☐	
Showers Yes ☐ No ☐ Free ☐ Paid ☐	
Enough Hot Water Yes ☐ No ☐	
Cleanliness:	

Amenities:

Pool	☐	Hot Tub	☐	Game Room	☐	Laundry	☐
Restaurant	☐	Pet-Friendly	☐	Dog Park	☐	Playground	☐
Shuffleboard	☐	Hiking	☐	Boating	☐	Fishing	☐
Horses	☐	Fitness Room	☐	Store	☐	Ice	☐
Firewood	☐		☐		☐		☐
Notes:							

Site Details for Site # _____:

RV Pad		Size/Access		Shade/Noise		Picnic Area	
Level	☐	Small	☐	No Shade	☐	Fire Ring	☐
Not Level	☐	Medium	☐	Partial Shade	☐	Fires Allowed	☐
Paved	☐	Large	☐	Full Shade	☐	Picnic Table	☐
Grass	☐	Tight Turns	☐	Quiet	☐	Good View	☐
Dirt	☐	Low Trees	☐	Light Noise	☐	Private	☐
Other	☐	Poor Roads	☐	Very Noisy	☐	No Privacy	☐

Safety:

Felt Very Safe ☐   Moderately Safe ☐   Felt Unsafe ☐

Wi-Fi:

Wi-Fi Available	☐
Poor Signal	☐
Good Signal	☐
Excellent Signal	☐
Notes:	

Notes:

_____
_____
_____
_____
_____
_____
_____

Who Was With Us? _____
_____
_____

People We Met: _____
_____
_____

Fun Things We Did: _____
_____
_____

Things to Remember For Next Time: _____
_____
_____
_____
_____

Favorite Memories: _____
_____
_____
_____
_____
_____
_____
_____

All About The Scenery: _____
_____
_____
_____
_____
_____

Area Around The Campground:

What Was the Weather Like? _____
_____
_____

Sightseeing/Activities:	Distance:	Fees/Contact Info:
_____	_____	_____
_____	_____	_____
_____	_____	_____
_____	_____	_____
_____	_____	_____

Nearby Restaurants: _____
_____
_____

Nearby Groceries: _____
_____
_____

Overall Thoughts About This Campground (Do you want
to revisit? Site # You Want to Reserve? Important Things
To Remember, etc.)

_____
_____
_____
_____
_____
_____
_____
_____

Notes, Lists, Drawings, Photos

Dates: _____ to _____

Campground: _____

Traveled From: _____ Miles: _____ Time: _____

Fees: _____ Pull-Through ☐ Back-In ☐

Hookups:

FHU	☐	W/E Only	☐
50 & 30 Amp	☐	30 Amp Only	☐
Dry Camp	☐	Dumping	☐
Notes:			

Restrooms/Showers:

Flush Toilets	Yes ☐	No ☐	
Showers Yes ☐ No ☐	Free ☐	Paid ☐	
Enough Hot Water	Yes ☐	No ☐	
Cleanliness:			

Amenities:

Pool	☐	Hot Tub	☐	Game Room	☐	Laundry	☐
Restaurant	☐	Pet-Friendly	☐	Dog Park	☐	Playground	☐
Shuffleboard	☐	Hiking	☐	Boating	☐	Fishing	☐
Horses	☐	Fitness Room	☐	Store	☐	Ice	☐
Firewood	☐		☐		☐		☐
Notes:							

Site Details for Site # _____:

RV Pad		Size/Access		Shade/Noise		Picnic Area	
Level	☐	Small	☐	No Shade	☐	Fire Ring	☐
Not Level	☐	Medium	☐	Partial Shade	☐	Fires Allowed	☐
Paved	☐	Large	☐	Full Shade	☐	Picnic Table	☐
Grass	☐	Tight Turns	☐	Quiet	☐	Good View	☐
Dirt	☐	Low Trees	☐	Light Noise	☐	Private	☐
Other	☐	Poor Roads	☐	Very Noisy	☐	No Privacy	☐

Safety:

Felt Very Safe ☐   Moderately Safe ☐   Felt Unsafe ☐

Wi-Fi:

Wi-Fi Available	☐
Poor Signal	☐
Good Signal	☐
Excellent Signal	☐
Notes:	

Notes:

_____
_____
_____
_____
_____
_____
_____
_____

Who Was With Us? _____

_____

_____

People We Met: _____

_____

_____

Fun Things We Did: _____

_____

_____

Things to Remember For Next Time: _____

_____

_____

_____

_____

Favorite Memories: _____

_____

_____

_____

_____

_____

_____

_____

All About The Scenery: _____

_____

_____

_____

_____

_____

Area Around The Campground:

What Was the Weather Like? _____
_____
_____

Sightseeing/Activities:	Distance:	Fees/Contact Info:
_____	_____	_____
_____	_____	_____
_____	_____	_____
_____	_____	_____
_____	_____	_____

Nearby Restaurants: _____
_____
_____

Nearby Groceries: _____
_____
_____

Overall Thoughts About This Campground (Do you want
to revisit? Site # You Want to Reserve? Important Things
To Remember, etc.)

_____
_____
_____
_____
_____
_____
_____

Notes, Lists, Drawings, Photos

Dates: _____ **to** _____

Campground: _____

Traveled From: _____ **Miles:** _____ **Time:** _____

Fees: _____ **Pull-Through** ☐ **Back-In** ☐

Hookups:

FHU	☐	W/E Only	☐
50 & 30 Amp	☐	30 Amp Only	☐
Dry Camp	☐	Dumping	☐
Notes:			

Restrooms/Showers:

Flush Toilets	Yes ☐	No ☐	
Showers Yes ☐	No ☐	Free ☐	Paid ☐
Enough Hot Water Yes ☐	No ☐		
Cleanliness:			

Amenities:

Pool	☐	Hot Tub	☐	Game Room	☐	Laundry	☐
Restaurant	☐	Pet-Friendly	☐	Dog Park	☐	Playground	☐
Shuffleboard	☐	Hiking	☐	Boating	☐	Fishing	☐
Horses	☐	Fitness Room	☐	Store	☐	Ice	☐
Firewood	☐		☐		☐		☐
Notes:							

Site Details for Site # _____:

RV Pad		Size/Access		Shade/Noise		Picnic Area	
Level	☐	Small	☐	No Shade	☐	Fire Ring	☐
Not Level	☐	Medium	☐	Partial Shade	☐	Fires Allowed	☐
Paved	☐	Large	☐	Full Shade	☐	Picnic Table	☐
Grass	☐	Tight Turns	☐	Quiet	☐	Good View	☐
Dirt	☐	Low Trees	☐	Light Noise	☐	Private	☐
Other	☐	Poor Roads	☐	Very Noisy	☐	No Privacy	☐

Safety:

Felt Very Safe ☐   Moderately Safe ☐   Felt Unsafe ☐

Wi-Fi:

Wi-Fi Available	☐
Poor Signal	☐
Good Signal	☐
Excellent Signal	☐
Notes:	

Notes:

_____
_____
_____
_____
_____
_____
_____
_____

Who Was With Us? _____
_____
_____

People We Met: _____
_____
_____

Fun Things We Did: _____
_____
_____

Things to Remember For Next Time: _____
_____
_____
_____
_____

Favorite Memories: _____
_____
_____
_____
_____
_____
_____
_____

All About The Scenery: _____
_____
_____
_____
_____
_____

Area Around The Campground:

What Was the Weather Like? _____
_____
_____

Sightseeing/Activities:	Distance:	Fees/Contact Info:
_____	_____	_____
_____	_____	_____
_____	_____	_____
_____	_____	_____
_____	_____	_____

Nearby Restaurants: _____
_____
_____

Nearby Groceries: _____
_____
_____

Overall Thoughts About This Campground (Do you want
to revisit? Site # You Want to Reserve? Important Things
To Remember, etc.)

_____
_____
_____
_____
_____
_____
_____
_____

Notes, Lists, Drawings, Photos

Dates:_____ **to** _____

Campground: _____

Traveled From: _____ **Miles:** _____ **Time:** _____

Fees: _____ **Pull-Through** ☐ **Back-In** ☐

Hookups:

FHU	☐	W/E Only	☐
50 & 30 Amp	☐	30 Amp Only	☐
Dry Camp	☐	Dumping	☐
Notes:			

Restrooms/Showers:

Flush Toilets	Yes ☐	No ☐
Showers Yes ☐	No ☐ Free ☐	Paid ☐
Enough Hot Water Yes ☐	No ☐	
Cleanliness:		

Amenities:

Pool	☐	Hot Tub	☐	Game Room	☐	Laundry	☐
Restaurant	☐	Pet-Friendly	☐	Dog Park	☐	Playground	☐
Shuffleboard	☐	Hiking	☐	Boating	☐	Fishing	☐
Horses	☐	Fitness Room	☐	Store	☐	Ice	☐
Firewood	☐		☐		☐		☐
Notes:							

Site Details for Site # _____:

RV Pad		Size/Access		Shade/Noise		Picnic Area	
Level	☐	Small	☐	No Shade	☐	Fire Ring	☐
Not Level	☐	Medium	☐	Partial Shade	☐	Fires Allowed	☐
Paved	☐	Large	☐	Full Shade	☐	Picnic Table	☐
Grass	☐	Tight Turns	☐	Quiet	☐	Good View	☐
Dirt	☐	Low Trees	☐	Light Noise	☐	Private	☐
Other	☐	Poor Roads	☐	Very Noisy	☐	No Privacy	☐

Safety:

Felt Very Safe ☐   Moderately Safe ☐   Felt Unsafe ☐

Wi-Fi:

Wi-Fi Available	☐
Poor Signal	☐
Good Signal	☐
Excellent Signal	☐
Notes:	

Notes:

_____
_____
_____
_____
_____
_____
_____
_____

Who Was With Us? _____

_____

_____

People We Met: _____

_____

_____

Fun Things We Did: _____

_____

_____

Things to Remember For Next Time: _____

_____

_____

_____

_____

Favorite Memories: _____

_____

_____

_____

_____

_____

_____

All About The Scenery: _____

_____

_____

_____

_____

_____

Area Around The Campground:

What Was the Weather Like? _____
_____
_____

Sightseeing/Activities:	Distance:	Fees/Contact Info:
_____	_____	_____
_____	_____	_____
_____	_____	_____
_____	_____	_____
_____	_____	_____

Nearby Restaurants: _____
_____
_____

Nearby Groceries: _____
_____
_____

Overall Thoughts About This Campground (Do you want
to revisit? Site # You Want to Reserve? Important Things
To Remember, etc.)

_____
_____
_____
_____
_____
_____
_____

Notes, Lists, Drawings, Photos

Dates: _____ to _____

Campground: _____

Traveled From: _____ Miles: _____ Time: _____

Fees: _____ Pull-Through ☐ Back-In ☐

Hookups:

FHU	☐	W/E Only	☐
50 & 30 Amp	☐	30 Amp Only	☐
Dry Camp	☐	Dumping	☐
Notes:			

Restrooms/Showers:

Flush Toilets Yes ☐ No ☐	
Showers Yes☐ No☐ Free☐ Paid☐	
Enough Hot Water Yes ☐ No ☐	
Cleanliness:	

Amenities:

Pool	☐	Hot Tub	☐	Game Room	☐	Laundry	☐
Restaurant	☐	Pet-Friendly	☐	Dog Park	☐	Playground	☐
Shuffleboard	☐	Hiking	☐	Boating	☐	Fishing	☐
Horses	☐	Fitness Room	☐	Store	☐	Ice	☐
Firewood	☐		☐		☐		☐
Notes:							

Site Details for Site # ____:

RV Pad		Size/Access		Shade/Noise		Picnic Area	
Level	☐	Small	☐	No Shade	☐	Fire Ring	☐
Not Level	☐	Medium	☐	Partial Shade	☐	Fires Allowed	☐
Paved	☐	Large	☐	Full Shade	☐	Picnic Table	☐
Grass	☐	Tight Turns	☐	Quiet	☐	Good View	☐
Dirt	☐	Low Trees	☐	Light Noise	☐	Private	☐
Other	☐	Poor Roads	☐	Very Noisy	☐	No Privacy	☐

Safety:

Felt Very Safe ☐   Moderately Safe ☐   Felt Unsafe ☐

Wi-Fi:

Wi-Fi Available	☐
Poor Signal	☐
Good Signal	☐
Excellent Signal	☐
Notes:	

Notes:

_____

_____

_____

_____

_____

_____

_____

Who Was With Us? _____

_____

_____

People We Met: _____

_____

_____

Fun Things We Did: _____

_____

_____

Things to Remember For Next Time: _____

_____

_____

_____

_____

Favorite Memories: _____

_____

_____

_____

_____

_____

_____

_____

All About The Scenery: _____

_____

_____

_____

_____

_____

Area Around The Campground:

What Was the Weather Like? _____
_____
_____

Sightseeing/Activities:	Distance:	Fees/Contact Info:
_____	_____	_____
_____	_____	_____
_____	_____	_____
_____	_____	_____
_____	_____	_____

Nearby Restaurants: _____
_____
_____

Nearby Groceries: _____
_____
_____

Overall Thoughts About This Campground (Do you want
to revisit? Site # You Want to Reserve? Important Things
To Remember, etc.)

_____
_____
_____
_____
_____
_____
_____

Notes, Lists, Drawings, Photos

Dates: _____ to _____

Campground: _____

Traveled From: _____ Miles: _____ Time: _____

Fees: _____ Pull-Through ☐ Back-In ☐

Hookups:

FHU	☐	W/E Only	☐
50 & 30 Amp	☐	30 Amp Only	☐
Dry Camp	☐	Dumping	☐
Notes:			

Restrooms/Showers:

Flush Toilets Yes ☐ No ☐	
Showers Yes ☐ No ☐ Free ☐ Paid ☐	
Enough Hot Water Yes ☐ No ☐	
Cleanliness:	

Amenities:

Pool	☐	Hot Tub	☐	Game Room	☐	Laundry	☐
Restaurant	☐	Pet-Friendly	☐	Dog Park	☐	Playground	☐
Shuffleboard	☐	Hiking	☐	Boating	☐	Fishing	☐
Horses	☐	Fitness Room	☐	Store	☐	Ice	☐
Firewood	☐		☐		☐		☐
Notes:							

Site Details for Site # _____:

RV Pad		Size/Access		Shade/Noise		Picnic Area	
Level	☐	Small	☐	No Shade	☐	Fire Ring	☐
Not Level	☐	Medium	☐	Partial Shade	☐	Fires Allowed	☐
Paved	☐	Large	☐	Full Shade	☐	Picnic Table	☐
Grass	☐	Tight Turns	☐	Quiet	☐	Good View	☐
Dirt	☐	Low Trees	☐	Light Noise	☐	Private	☐
Other	☐	Poor Roads	☐	Very Noisy	☐	No Privacy	☐

Safety:

Felt Very Safe ☐   Moderately Safe ☐   Felt Unsafe ☐

Wi-Fi:

Wi-Fi Available	☐
Poor Signal	☐
Good Signal	☐
Excellent Signal	☐
Notes:	

Notes:

_____
_____
_____
_____
_____
_____
_____
_____

Who Was With Us? _____
_____
_____

People We Met: _____
_____
_____

Fun Things We Did: _____
_____
_____

Things to Remember For Next Time: _____
_____
_____
_____
_____

Favorite Memories: _____
_____
_____
_____
_____
_____
_____

All About The Scenery: _____
_____
_____
_____
_____
_____

Area Around The Campground:

What Was the Weather Like? _____
_____
_____

Sightseeing/Activities:	Distance:	Fees/Contact Info:
_____	_____	_____
_____	_____	_____
_____	_____	_____
_____	_____	_____
_____	_____	_____

Nearby Restaurants: _____
_____
_____

Nearby Groceries: _____
_____
_____

Overall Thoughts About This Campground (Do you want
to revisit? Site # You Want to Reserve? Important Things
To Remember, etc.)

_____
_____
_____
_____
_____
_____
_____
_____

Notes, Lists, Drawings, Photos

Dates: _____ **to** _____

Campground: _____

Traveled From: _____ **Miles:** ____ **Time:** ____

Fees: _____ **Pull-Through** ☐ **Back-In** ☐

Hookups:

FHU	☐	W/E Only	☐
50 & 30 Amp	☐	30 Amp Only	☐
Dry Camp	☐	Dumping	☐
Notes:			

Restrooms/Showers:

Flush Toilets	Yes ☐	No ☐	
Showers Yes ☐ No ☐	Free ☐	Paid ☐	
Enough Hot Water Yes ☐	No ☐		
Cleanliness:			

Amenities:

Pool	☐	Hot Tub	☐	Game Room	☐	Laundry	☐
Restaurant	☐	Pet-Friendly	☐	Dog Park	☐	Playground	☐
Shuffleboard	☐	Hiking	☐	Boating	☐	Fishing	☐
Horses	☐	Fitness Room	☐	Store	☐	Ice	☐
Firewood	☐		☐		☐		☐
Notes:							

Site Details for Site # ____:

RV Pad		Size/Access		Shade/Noise		Picnic Area	
Level	☐	Small	☐	No Shade	☐	Fire Ring	☐
Not Level	☐	Medium	☐	Partial Shade	☐	Fires Allowed	☐
Paved	☐	Large	☐	Full Shade	☐	Picnic Table	☐
Grass	☐	Tight Turns	☐	Quiet	☐	Good View	☐
Dirt	☐	Low Trees	☐	Light Noise	☐	Private	☐
Other	☐	Poor Roads	☐	Very Noisy	☐	No Privacy	☐

Safety:

Felt Very Safe ☐   Moderately Safe ☐   Felt Unsafe ☐

Wi-Fi:

Wi-Fi Available	☐
Poor Signal	☐
Good Signal	☐
Excellent Signal	☐
Notes:	

Notes:

_____
_____
_____
_____
_____
_____
_____
_____

Who Was With Us? _____

_____

_____

People We Met: _____

_____

_____

Fun Things We Did: _____

_____

_____

Things to Remember For Next Time: _____

_____

_____

_____

_____

Favorite Memories: _____

_____

_____

_____

_____

_____

_____

All About The Scenery: _____

_____

_____

_____

_____

Area Around The Campground:

What Was the Weather Like? _____
_____
_____

Sightseeing/Activities:	Distance:	Fees/Contact Info:
_____	_____	_____
_____	_____	_____
_____	_____	_____
_____	_____	_____
_____	_____	_____

Nearby Restaurants: _____
_____
_____

Nearby Groceries: _____
_____
_____

Overall Thoughts About This Campground (Do you want
to revisit? Site # You Want to Reserve? Important Things
To Remember, etc.)

_____
_____
_____
_____
_____
_____
_____
_____

Notes, Lists, Drawings, Photos

Dates: _____ **to** _____

Campground: _____

Traveled From: _____ **Miles:** _____ **Time:** _____

Fees: _____ **Pull-Through** ☐ **Back-In** ☐

Hookups:

FHU	☐	W/E Only	☐
50 & 30 Amp	☐	30 Amp Only	☐
Dry Camp	☐	Dumping	☐
Notes:			

Restrooms/Showers:

Flush Toilets	Yes ☐	No ☐	
Showers Yes ☐	No ☐	Free ☐	Paid ☐
Enough Hot Water	Yes ☐	No ☐	
Cleanliness:			

Amenities:

Pool	☐	Hot Tub	☐	Game Room	☐	Laundry	☐
Restaurant	☐	Pet-Friendly	☐	Dog Park	☐	Playground	☐
Shuffleboard	☐	Hiking	☐	Boating	☐	Fishing	☐
Horses	☐	Fitness Room	☐	Store	☐	Ice	☐
Firewood	☐		☐		☐		☐
Notes:							

Site Details for Site # _____:

RV Pad		Size/Access		Shade/Noise		Picnic Area	
Level	☐	Small	☐	No Shade	☐	Fire Ring	☐
Not Level	☐	Medium	☐	Partial Shade	☐	Fires Allowed	☐
Paved	☐	Large	☐	Full Shade	☐	Picnic Table	☐
Grass	☐	Tight Turns	☐	Quiet	☐	Good View	☐
Dirt	☐	Low Trees	☐	Light Noise	☐	Private	☐
Other	☐	Poor Roads	☐	Very Noisy	☐	No Privacy	☐

Safety:

Felt Very Safe ☐   Moderately Safe ☐   Felt Unsafe ☐

Wi-Fi:

Wi-Fi Available	☐
Poor Signal	☐
Good Signal	☐
Excellent Signal	☐
Notes:	

Notes:

_____
_____
_____
_____
_____
_____
_____

Who Was With Us? _____

_____

_____

People We Met: _____

_____

_____

Fun Things We Did: _____

_____

_____

Things to Remember For Next Time: _____

_____

_____

_____

_____

Favorite Memories: _____

_____

_____

_____

_____

_____

_____

_____

All About The Scenery: _____

_____

_____

_____

_____

_____

Area Around The Campground:

What Was the Weather Like? _____
_____
_____

Sightseeing/Activities:	Distance:	Fees/Contact Info:
_____	_____	_____
_____	_____	_____
_____	_____	_____
_____	_____	_____
_____	_____	_____

Nearby Restaurants: _____
_____
_____

Nearby Groceries: _____
_____
_____

Overall Thoughts About This Campground (Do you want
to revisit? Site # You Want to Reserve? Important Things
To Remember, etc.)

_____
_____
_____
_____
_____
_____
_____
_____

Notes, Lists, Drawings, Photos

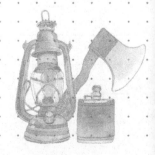

Trip #30

Dates: _____ to _____

Campground: _____

Traveled From: _____ Miles: _____ Time: _____

Fees: _____ Pull-Through ☐ Back-In ☐

Hookups:

FHU	☐	W/E Only	☐
50 & 30 Amp	☐	30 Amp Only	☐
Dry Camp	☐	Dumping	☐
Notes:			

Restrooms/Showers:

Flush Toilets		Yes ☐		No ☐	
Showers Yes ☐	No ☐		Free ☐	Paid ☐	
Enough Hot Water	Yes ☐		No ☐		
Cleanliness:					

Amenities:

Pool	☐	Hot Tub	☐	Game Room	☐	Laundry	☐
Restaurant	☐	Pet-Friendly	☐	Dog Park	☐	Playground	☐
Shuffleboard	☐	Hiking	☐	Boating	☐	Fishing	☐
Horses	☐	Fitness Room	☐	Store	☐	Ice	☐
Firewood	☐		☐		☐		☐
Notes:							

Site Details for Site # _____:

RV Pad		Size/Access		Shade/Noise		Picnic Area	
Level	☐	Small	☐	No Shade	☐	Fire Ring	☐
Not Level	☐	Medium	☐	Partial Shade	☐	Fires Allowed	☐
Paved	☐	Large	☐	Full Shade	☐	Picnic Table	☐
Grass	☐	Tight Turns	☐	Quiet	☐	Good View	☐
Dirt	☐	Low Trees	☐	Light Noise	☐	Private	☐
Other	☐	Poor Roads	☐	Very Noisy	☐	No Privacy	☐

Safety:

Felt Very Safe ☐   Moderately Safe ☐   Felt Unsafe ☐

Wi-Fi:

Wi-Fi Available	☐
Poor Signal	☐
Good Signal	☐
Excellent Signal	☐
Notes:	

Notes:

_____
_____
_____
_____
_____
_____
_____
_____
_____

Who Was With Us? _____
_____
_____

People We Met: _____
_____
_____

Fun Things We Did: _____
_____
_____

Things to Remember For Next Time: _____
_____
_____
_____
_____

Favorite Memories: _____
_____
_____
_____
_____
_____
_____
_____

All About The Scenery: _____
_____
_____
_____
_____
_____

Area Around The Campground:

What Was the Weather Like? _____
_____
_____

Sightseeing/Activities:	Distance:	Fees/Contact Info:
_____	_____	_____
_____	_____	_____
_____	_____	_____
_____	_____	_____
_____	_____	_____

Nearby Restaurants: _____
_____
_____

Nearby Groceries: _____
_____
_____

Overall Thoughts About This Campground (Do you want
to revisit? Site # You Want to Reserve? Important Things
To Remember, etc.)

_____
_____
_____
_____
_____
_____
_____
_____

Notes, Lists, Drawings, Photos

Tent Camping Checklist

Campsite

- Tent ☐
- Sleeping Bags ☐
- Sleeping Pads ☐
- Pillow ☐
- Flashlights ☐
- Camp Chairs ☐
- Camp Table ☐
- Lantern ☐
- Hammock ☐
- Tarp ☐
- Screen House ☐
- Firewood ☐
- Camp Ring ☐
- Tablecloth & Clips ☐
- Clothesline ☐
- ☐
- ☐
- ☐
- ☐

Health/Hygiene

- First Aid Kit ☐
- Prescription Meds ☐
- Toilet Paper ☐
- Toothbrush/paste ☐
- Toiletry Kit ☐
- Quick Dry Towel ☐
- Menstrual Products ☐
- Insect Repellent ☐
- Lip Balm ☐
- Sunscreen ☐
- Ibuprofen ☐
- Antiseptic Wipes ☐
- Mirror/Brush/Comb ☐
- Cosmetics ☐
- Spare Glasses ☐
- Deodorant ☐
- ☐
- ☐
- ☐

Cooking

- Stove & Fuel ☐
- Matches/Lighter ☐
- Cook Pots ☐
- Potholder ☐
- Frying Pan ☐
- Cooking Utensils ☐
- Eating Utensils ☐
- Bottle/Can Opener ☐
- Sharp Knife ☐
- Plates/Mugs ☐
- Cutting Board ☐
- Cooler ☐
- Water Bottles ☐
- Wash Tub & Sponge ☐
- Trash Bags ☐
- Dish Towel ☐
- Griddle ☐
- Dutch Oven ☐
- Charcoal ☐
- Coffee/Tea Pot ☐
- Roasting Forks ☐
- Food Containers ☐
- Large Water Jugs ☐
- Bins for Storage ☐
- Dish Soap ☐
- ☐
- ☐
- ☐

Clothing

- Long Sleeve Shirts ☐
- T-Shirts ☐
- Shorts/Pants ☐
- Boots/Shoes ☐
- Socks ☐
- Sleepwear ☐
- Underwear ☐
- Jacket ☐
- Rainwear ☐
- Long Underwear ☐
- Gloves/Mittens ☐
- Warm Hat ☐
- Sun Hat ☐
- Sunglasses ☐
- Sandals ☐
- Swimsuit ☐
- ☐
- ☐
- ☐

Tools & Repairs

- Multi Tool ☐
- Duct Tape ☐
- Cord ☐
- Tent Repair Kit ☐
- Saw/Axe ☐
- Broom/Dustpan ☐
- Screwdriver ☐
- Shovel ☐
- Hammer/Mallet ☐
- ☐
- ☐
- ☐

Personal Items

- Credit Card/Cash ☐
- ID/ Driver's License ☐
- Phone & Charger ☐
- Reservation Info ☐
- ☐
- ☐
- ☐

Extras

- Binoculars ☐
- Navigation Tools ☐
- Field Guides ☐
- Notebook/Pen ☐
- Games/Toys/Books ☐
- Dog Gear ☐
- Dry Bags, Bins ☐
- Star Chart ☐
- Hammer/Mallet ☐
- ☐
- ☐

RV Checklist

Essentials

- [ ] Surge Protector
- [ ] Electric Adapters
- [ ] Toilet Chemicals
- [ ] Sewer Kit
- [ ] RV Toilet Paper
- [ ] Water Pressure Regulator
- [ ] Drinking Water Hose
- [ ] Leveling Blocks
- [ ] Tire Pressure Gauge
- [ ] Extension Cords
- [ ] Wheel Chocks
- [ ] Shovel
- [ ] Duct Tape
- [ ] Cotter Pins
- [ ] Oil & Trans. Fluid
- [ ] Flashlight
- [ ] Jumper Cables
- [ ] Emergency Road Kit
- [ ] Fire Extinguisher
- [ ] Folder w/ Important Documents
- [ ]

Clothing & Bedroom

- [ ] Sheets/Blankets
- [ ] Pillows
- [ ] Towels
- [ ] Alarm Clock
- [ ] Clothes Hangers
- [ ] Pants/Shorts
- [ ] Shirts
- [ ] Hat
- [ ] Socks/Underwear
- [ ] Swimsuit
- [ ] Rain Gear
- [ ] Boots/Shoes
- [ ] Sweatshirt/Jacket
- [ ] Sewing Kit
- [ ] Laundry Bag
- [ ] Heavy Coat
- [ ]
- [ ]

Food Staples

- [ ] Batter Mixes
- [ ] Butter
- [ ] Fruits/Vegetables
- [ ] Hot Dogs
- [ ] Condiments
- [ ] Cereal
- [ ] Eggs
- [ ] Salt/Pepper/Spices
- [ ] Bread
- [ ] S'More Ingredients
- [ ] Flour, Sugar, etc.
- [ ] Canned Foods
- [ ] Snacks
- [ ] Peanut Butter
- [ ] Jelly
- [ ] Soup
- [ ] Cooking Oil/Spray
- [ ]
- [ ]
- [ ]

Kitchen Items

- [ ] Water Bottles
- [ ] Utensils/Knives
- [ ] Plates/Bowls/Cups
- [ ] Can Opener
- [ ] Tongs/Skewers
- [ ] Griddle
- [ ] Dish Soap
- [ ] Paper Towels
- [ ] Trash Bags
- [ ] Plastic Wrap/Bags
- [ ] Pot Holders/Towels
- [ ] Skillet/Sauce Pan
- [ ] Matches/Lighter
- [ ] Storage Containers
- [ ] Cooler
- [ ]
- [ ]
- [ ]

Personal/Toiletries

- [ ] Phone/Charger
- [ ] Cash/Credit Cards
- [ ] Reservations
- [ ] First Aid Kit
- [ ] Sunscreen
- [ ] Bug Spray
- [ ] Batteries
- [ ] Watch/Clock
- [ ] Medications
- [ ] Glasses/Contacts
- [ ] Sunglasses
- [ ] Maps/Directories
- [ ] Shampoo/Soap
- [ ] Bruch/Comb
- [ ] Toothbrush/Paste
- [ ] Deodorant
- [ ] Hair Ties
- [ ] Lotion
- [ ] Makeup
- [ ] Razor
- [ ] Nail Clippers
- [ ]
- [ ]
- [ ]
- [ ]

Recreation

- [ ] Camera
- [ ] Firewood
- [ ] Camping Chairs
- [ ] Hammock
- [ ] Games/Toys/Books
- [ ] Dog Gear
- [ ] Fishing Gear
- [ ] Binoculars
- [ ] Playing Cards
- [ ] Musical Instrument
- [ ] Flotation Devices
- [ ] Laptop
- [ ] Notepad/Pen
- [ ]

Notes, Lists, Drawings, Photos

Notes, Lists, Drawings, Photos

Made in United States
Orlando, FL
09 November 2021

10310068R00075